Level 2

The Nature Kid's Guide to CATERPILLARS

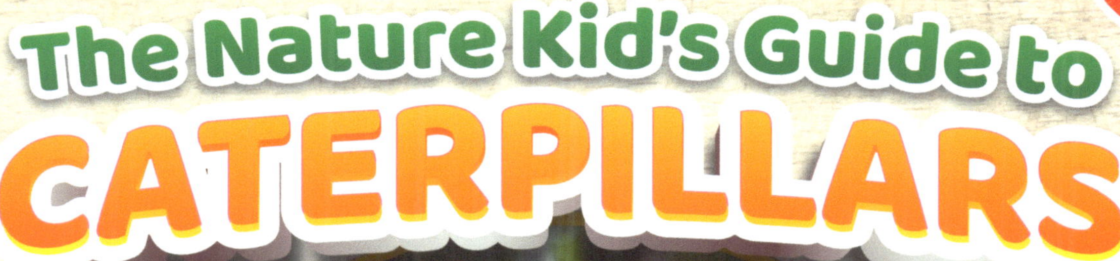

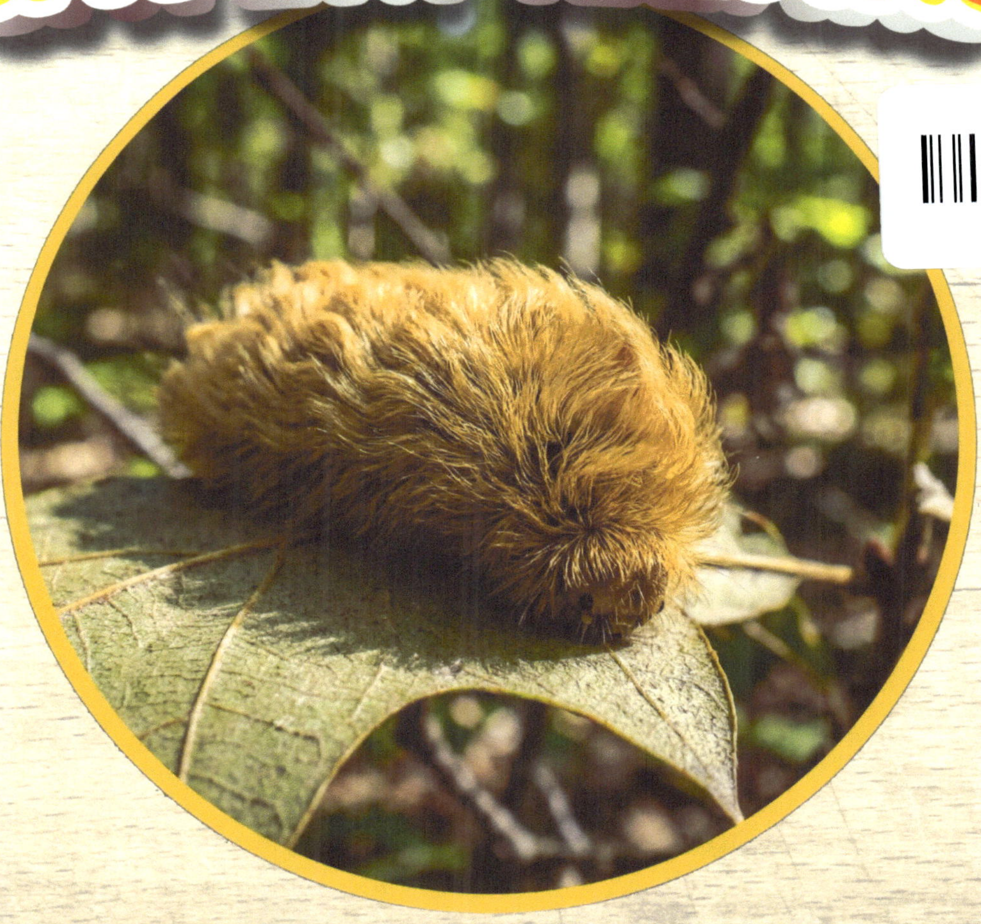

DAVID ANDERSON

LP Media Inc. Publishing
Text copyright © 2026 by LP Media Inc.
All rights reserved.

For information address LP Media Inc. Publishing,
30012 Variolite St NW, Princeton MN 55371
www.lpmedia.org

Publication Data

Caterpillars
The Nature Kid's Guide to Caterpillars — First edition.

Summary: "Learn all about Caterpillars, the Nature Kid Way"
— Provided by publisher.

ISBN: 979-8-89818-206-9

[1. Caterpillars – Non-Fiction] I. Title.

Title: The Nature Kid's Guide to Caterpillars

CONTENTS

EAT AND GROW

4

Crunch! A monarch caterpillar chews right through a big green leaf.

Caterpillars are baby butterflies and moths. They hatch from tiny eggs laid on leaves. Each one has a soft, long body with many legs.

Most caterpillars have six true legs near the head. They also have fleshy bumps called prolegs that help them hold on tight to branches and stems.

A caterpillar's main job is simple: eat and grow. It needs lots of food to get big. One day, this hungry crawler will change into something truly amazing.

MUNCHING MACHINES

Chomp! A fat green caterpillar tears off a chunk of juicy leaf.

Caterpillars are eating machines. Some eat three times their body weight in just one day! Their strong jaws cut leaves like tiny scissors.

Many caterpillars eat only one kind of plant. Tiny sensors on their mouths and feet help them find the right one. If the plant is wrong, they simply walk away.

As a caterpillar eats, it grows fast. Too fast. Its skin gets tight, so it sheds the old skin. This is called **molting**, and most caterpillars do it four or five times.

SURVIVAL SECRETS

FUN FACT!

8

Hiss! A caterpillar puffs up its body to scare a hungry bird.

Many animals want to eat caterpillars. Birds, wasps, and spiders hunt them every day. So caterpillars need smart ways to stay safe.

Some caterpillars blend in perfectly with leaves or twigs. Others have bright colors that shout, stay away! These bold colors often mean they taste terrible.

A few caterpillars puff up to look much bigger than they really are. Some drop off branches and play dead on the ground.

Each clever trick gives them a better chance to survive another day.

MAGICAL CHANGES

A butterfly can remember some things it learned as a caterpillar — even after its brain completely changed!

Crack! A monarch butterfly pushes out of its tiny green case.

When a caterpillar is big enough, something amazing begins. It hangs from a branch or leaf and forms a hard shell called a **chrysalis**.

Inside, the caterpillar's body breaks down completely. It slowly rebuilds into a butterfly or moth. This incredible change is called **metamorphosis**.

After days or weeks, the shell finally splits open. A new butterfly climbs out and dries its crumpled wings. Then it flies away into the sky, ready for a whole new life.

MONARCH MAGIC

FUN FACT!

Monarch butterflies migrate up to 3,000 miles — that's like walking from New York to California!

Munch! A striped monarch caterpillar nibbles on milkweed all day.

Monarch caterpillars have bold black, white, and yellow stripes. These bright bands warn birds to stay far away. The colors tell predators that this caterpillar is not safe to eat.

Monarchs only eat milkweed leaves. The milkweed contains a poison that builds up in their bodies, making them taste awful to birds. This is their secret shield.

Monarch caterpillars live in fields and meadows across North America. When they grow up, they become the famous orange and black butterfly that travels thousands of miles.

SURVIVAL SWITCH

Poof! A swallowtail shoots out smelly orange horns from its head.

Swallowtail caterpillars have a super cool trick. When scared, they push out two orange horns from behind their head. These horns smell terrible — like rotting fruit — and scare away enemies.

Young swallowtails look exactly like bird droppings. Gross, but clever! This disguise helps them hide in plain sight. As they grow bigger, they turn bright green.

Some swallowtails also have big fake eye spots on their bodies. These spots make them look like a small snake. Most birds take one look and fly away fast!

HARMLESS HORNS

The royal walnut moth has wings six inches wide — but it never eats because it has no working mouth!

Rip! A scary horned caterpillar tears through a leaf with its big jaws.

The hickory horned devil looks absolutely fierce. It has curved red and black horns on its head. Its body can grow as long as a hot dog — nearly six inches!

But do not worry. This big caterpillar is totally harmless. It cannot sting or bite you at all. Its scary look is just a bluff to fool predators.

Hickory horned devils live in forests in the eastern United States. They munch on hickory, walnut, and other tree leaves all summer long. Then they become the beautiful royal walnut moth.

FUZZY DANGER

Scratch! A fluffy caterpillar hides sharp stingers under its soft fur.

The puss caterpillar looks like a tiny furry pet. Its long soft hairs hang down like a little wig. But looks can trick you.

Under that fluffy coat are sharp, venomous spines. If you touch them, they break off in your skin and release poison. The sting can really, really hurt.

Puss caterpillars live in the southern United States. They rest on tree trunks and hide under leaves. Always look, but never touch a fuzzy caterpillar you find outside!

SPINY STINGERS

Zing! A bright green caterpillar stings a bird with its sharp spines.

Io moth caterpillars are bright green with red and white stripes. Rows of sharp spines stick up along their backs like tiny cactus needles. Those spines are full of venom.

If something brushes against them, the spines poke in instantly. They leave a burning, itchy rash that can last for hours. Even a light touch can set them off.

Young io caterpillars live in groups for safety. They eat leaves from many kinds of trees. As adults, they become lovely tan and yellow moths with huge eye spots on their wings.

WOOLLY WONDERS

Thud! A fuzzy woolly bear caterpillar drops and rolls into a ball.

Woolly bears are some of the best known caterpillars in North America. They have fuzzy black and brown bands around their body. You can often spot them crossing roads in fall.

Some people think woolly bears predict winter weather. They say wider brown bands mean a mild winter ahead. But this is just a fun old story, not real science.

When scared, a woolly bear curls up into a tight ball and stays perfectly still. It waits until the danger passes. In spring, it becomes the orange and cream isabella tiger moth.

HAWK HULKS

24

Plop! A huge green caterpillar drops off a branch onto a garden plant.

Hawk moth caterpillars are big and chunky. Most are green or brown with diagonal stripes on their sides. They have a pointed horn on their rear end that looks sharp but is harmless.

People often call them hornworms. You might spot one munching in a vegetable garden. They love tomato and pepper plants — gardeners do not love them back!

Hawk moth caterpillars grow very large, very fast. Some wiggle and thrash wildly when picked up. They become hawk moths that can hover in place like tiny hummingbirds.

SLUGGISH SLIDERS

Some slug caterpillar cocoons have a built-in escape hatch — a tiny lid that pops open for the moth!

Slurp! A flat little caterpillar slides along a leaf like a slug.

Slug caterpillars got their name from the way they move. They glide smoothly over leaves, just like real slugs. Their prolegs are hidden under their flat, oval bodies.

These caterpillars slide along on a thin layer of sticky silk they make as they go. This makes them very quiet and hard to spot among the leaves.

Some slug caterpillars have bright colors and stinging spines. Others look exactly like leaves or tree bark. Both kinds live on trees in warm forests around the world.

CINNABAR STRIPES

Cinnabar moths were brought to America and Australia on purpose — to help control poisonous ragwort weeds!

Nibble! A bold striped caterpillar chews on a yellow ragwort flower.

Cinnabar moth caterpillars are easy to spot. They have bold orange and black stripes like tiny tigers. These warning colors tell predators not to eat them.

These caterpillars love to eat ragwort plants. Ragwort is a weed that poisons horses and cows. But cinnabar caterpillars can eat it safely and store the toxins in their own bodies.

Cinnabar caterpillars often feed in large, hungry groups. They can strip a whole plant bare in just a few days. They live across Europe and parts of North America.

ATLAS GIANTS

Snap! A fat caterpillar covered in white powder eats a leaf.

Atlas moth caterpillars are some of the biggest in the world. They are pale green with a dusty white waxy coating that makes them look frosted. This waxy layer helps protect their soft skin from drying out.

These giant caterpillars live in the tropical forests of Asia. They feed on many kinds of trees and eat constantly. They grow over four inches long — as big as your hand!

When it is time to change, they spin a big silk **cocoon**. The atlas moth that emerges has enormous wings. Its wingspan can reach eleven inches wide!

SADDLEBACK STING

Zap! A small brown and green caterpillar stings with both ends.

The saddleback caterpillar is small but fierce. It is brown with a bright green patch on its back that looks just like a tiny saddle. Two purple spots sit in the middle like decorations.

Sharp spines stick out from both ends of its body. These spines have venom that causes a painful sting, like touching a hot needle.

Saddleback caterpillars live in eastern North America. They rest on the undersides of tree leaves where they are hard to see. Watch out if you spot one — admire it from a distance!

FLUFFY FAKERS

34

Rustle! A fuzzy caterpillar that looks like soft fur hides a secret.

Flannel moth caterpillars come in many shapes and colors. Some look like tiny cotton balls. Others are fuzzy and golden like little wigs or tufts of fur.

But all of them share a painful secret. Under that soft, fluffy look are rows of hidden spines. If you touch one, the spines sting and leave an itchy rash.

These caterpillars live across North and South America on many kinds of trees. Their fluffy coats help them blend in with bark and moss. Always admire fuzzy caterpillars from a safe distance — never touch!

FUZZY HELPERS

Scientists count caterpillars to check how healthy a forest is — more caterpillars means a healthier ecosystem!

36

Wiggle! A woolly bear caterpillar crawls slowly down a branch.

Caterpillars are important to the whole world. They are food for birds, frogs, lizards, and many other animals. Without caterpillars, these creatures would go hungry.

When caterpillars become butterflies and moths, they help plants grow. They carry **pollen** from flower to flower as they drink nectar. This helps new plants sprout and spread.

But some caterpillars are in danger today. People cut down forests and spray chemicals that harm them. We can help by planting wildflowers, avoiding pesticides, and keeping wild places safe.

MIRACLE MAKERS
FUN FACT!
There are over 180,000 kinds of butterflies and moths — and every single one started life as a tiny caterpillar!

Whirr! A brand new moth stretches its wings for the first time.

Caterpillars are all around us! Look under leaves, not on top. Most caterpillars hide on the shady underside. Check milkweed, oak leaves, and wild plants along garden edges.

You can make your yard caterpillar friendly too. Plant native flowers and shrubs since many caterpillars will only eat certain plants. Leave a few wild weedy corners — a messy patch of garden is often a caterpillar's favorite spot.

When you find one, just watch. Notice how it moves, eats, and grips the stem. That small crawler is quietly preparing to become something truly beautiful.

GLOSSARY

chrysalis
The hard shell a caterpillar forms to change into a butterfly.

cocoon
A silk case some caterpillars spin before they change.

metamorphosis
The big change from caterpillar to butterfly or moth.

molting
When a caterpillar sheds its old skin to grow bigger.

pollen
Tiny powder from flowers that helps plants make seeds.